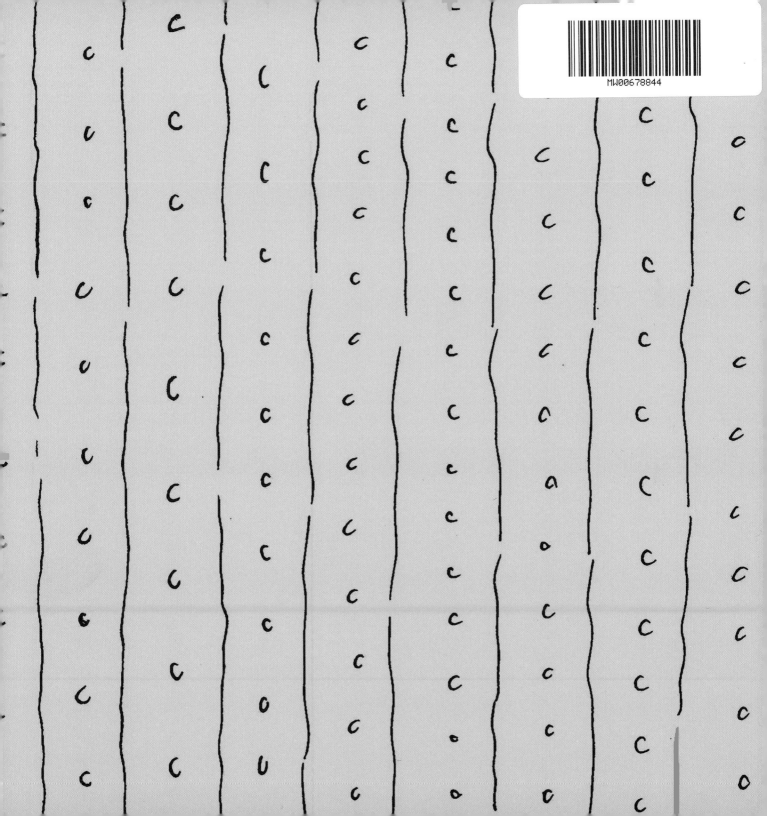

What Is a Book?

From the Author

Thirty years ago, New Zealander Dame Marie Clay took Reading Recovery® to the United States, where it quickly became a homegrown product helping young readers at risk. To celebrate thirty years of child empowerment, it seems appropriate that another New Zealander who sees the United States as a second home should write a book for the 2015 National Reading Recovery and Literacy Conference. With award-winning illustrator Philip Webb and educational publisher Raymond Yuen of Hameray, I am very happy to offer you What Is a Book?

The author's royalty is donated to the Reading Recovery Council of North America, whose work is above price.

With love ♡ Joy Cowley

What Is a Book?

Written By Joy Cowley
Illustrated by Philip Webb

HAMERAY
PUBLISHING GROUP

What is a book?

A book can be a mat
for a cat.

A book can be a house
for a mouse.

But what is a book
for you and for me?
A book has words
that make a story.

4

A story can be fiction.

A story can be true.

I can read a story.

You can read it, too.

This book has a shark
swimming in the sea.
The shark's teeth are sharp.
Will it bite me?

No, it can't bite me! Look!
It's just a story in a book.

A spaceship hits a meteor
and the engine smashes.
Will I be sad
if the spaceship crashes?

No, I won't be sad. Look!
It's just a story in a book.

9

But a story might
give us a fright.
It might wake us
in the night.

Do you like scary stories?

10

A monster can be scary.
So can a bear
that is big and hairy.

11

If you don't like a scary book,
please, please, do not look
at the last page in this book.

Close it now. Go away.
Please, please,
go out and play.

Stop! Stop! Do not look
at the last page in this book!
Stop right now.
I'm warning you!

14

The last page
will frighten you!

About The Author

Joy Cowley is a mother, grandmother, and great-grandmother who has been learning from children all her life. She began writing for children when she was sixteen, with an after-school job as editor of the children's page in a local newspaper. Her focus on early reading began twelve years later with stories for her son who was a reluctant reader. With the support and encouragement of classroom teachers, she worked one on one with children who taught her that reading texts must have meaning, and that stories need to be entertaining and child-centered. Teachers asked that the stories be published. The first set of early reading books, including the original *Mrs. Wishy-Washy*, was published in 1980 and instantly went global. Since then, there have been hundreds of titles, many of which have been used by Reading Recovery teachers.

Her connection with Reading Recovery began in New Zealand with friend Dame Marie Clay, who brought Reading Recovery to the United States. This book, published by Hameray, is in celebration of Marie Clay's work in the United States, and it comes with gratitude for all that Reading Recovery teachers do for children.

A lifetime of writing collects a few awards. A full list is on Joy's website: www.joycowley.com. Among these are four awards specifically for writing early reading material: OBE (Order of the British Empire), DCNZM (Dame Commander of the New Zealand Order of Merit), the Maryann Manning Medal for literacy, and an Hon. D.Litt. from Massey University. Joy is grateful for these but does not use titles. To do so would create a barrier between her and the children who greet her simply with "Hi, Joy!"

Published in the United States of America
by the Hameray Publishing Group, Inc.

Publisher: Raymond Yuen
Book Illustrator: Philip Webb
Book Designer: Anita Adams

ISBN: 978-1-62817-554-7

Printed in Singapore

1 2 3 4 5 6 CP 20 19 18 17 16 15

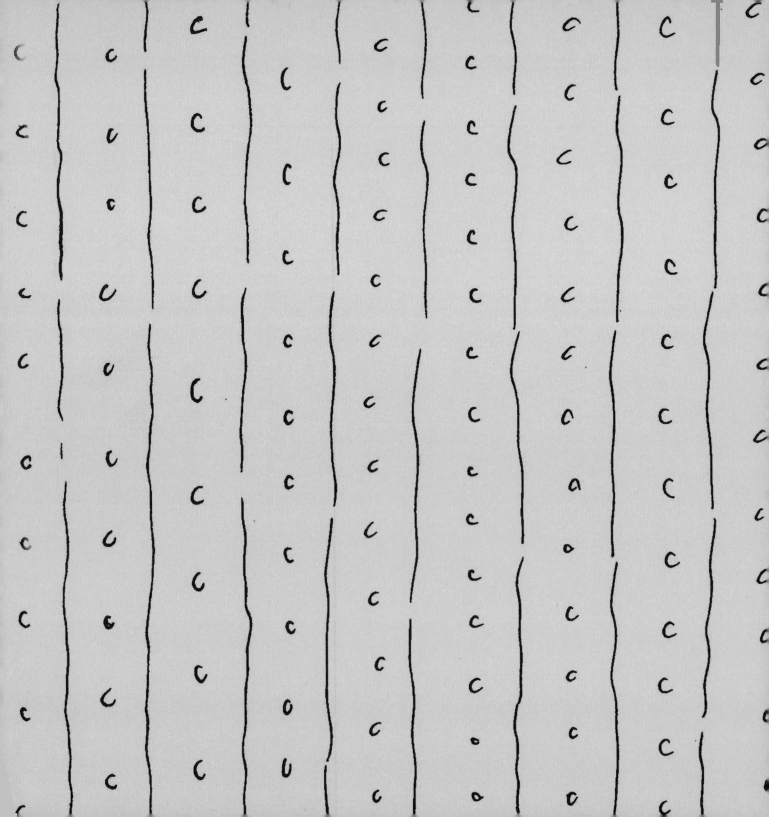